Vakare Rimkute

ADHD & AUTISM COOKBOOK: Flavorful Solutions for Nurturing Neurological Wellness through Wholesome Recipes

Dedicated to individuals navigating the incredible road of ADHD and Autism. May each recipe in this cookbook bring you joy, encourage connection, and nourish not just your body but also your soul. Here's to a future where every meal is a celebration of each person's unique qualities and a monument to their perseverance and beauty.

Contents

1.
    1.
    2.
2.
    1.
    2.
    3.
    4.
3.
    1.
    2.

3.

4.

Chapter 1: Introduction

What is ADHD & Autism:

ADHD (Attention Deficit Hyperactivity Disorder) and Autism Spectrum Disorder (ASD) are two distinct neurological conditions that affect individuals in different ways. Here's a quick rundown of each:

ADHD (Attention Deficit Hyperactivity Disorder):

ADHD is a neurodevelopmental disorder characterized by persistent patterns of inattention, hyperactivity, and impulsivity that can interfere with daily functioning or development. There are three main types of ADHD:

1. **Predominantly Inattentive Presentation:** Individuals with this type may have difficulty sustaining attention, being organized, and completing tasks. They may seem forgetful and easily distracted.

2. **Predominantly Hyperactive-Impulsive Presentation**: This type involves excessive fidgeting, restlessness, impulsive behaviour, and difficulty waiting or taking turns.

3. **Combined Presentation**: This type involves a combination of both inattentive and hyperactive-impulsive symptoms.

ADHD is most commonly diagnosed in childhood, although symptoms can last into adolescence and adulthood. While precise aetiology is unknown, a mix of genetic, environmental, and neurological variables are thought to have a role in its development. Treatment is usually multimodal, involving behavioural therapies, psychoeducation, and, in some situations, medication.

Autism Spectrum Disorder (ASD):

ASD is a complex neurodevelopmental condition characterized by a range of challenges in social interaction, communication, and repetitive behaviours. The term "spectrum" reflects the wide variation in symptoms and severity among individuals with ASD. Some common characteristics include:

1. **Social Challenge**s: Difficulty with social interactions, including understanding and responding to social cues, making eye contact, and forming relationships.

2. **Communication Difficulties**: Challenges in verbal and nonverbal communication, such as delayed speech development, limited use of gestures, and difficulty maintaining conversations.

3. **Repetitive Behaviors**: Engaging in repetitive movements or activities, insistence on sameness, and intense interest in specific topics.

ASD is frequently diagnosed in childhood, however, the severity of symptoms can vary greatly. The specific aetiology of ASD is unknown, however, it is thought to be a mix of genetic and environmental factors. Early intervention, behavioural treatments, speech therapy, and educational assistance are all frequent components of ASD treatment.

Importance of Diet in Managing Symptoms:

1. **Nutrient Intake:**
   - Adequate intake of essential nutrients, such as omega-3 fatty acids, vitamins, and minerals, is crucial for brain development and function. Deficiencies in these nutrients have been linked to behavioural and cognitive issues.

2. **Inflammation Reduction**:
   - Certain dietary patterns may contribute to inflammation, which is thought to play a role in various neurological disorders. Anti-inflammatory diets, rich in fruits, vegetables, and omega-3 fatty acids, may help reduce inflammation in the body and brain.

3. **Blood Sugar Stability**:

- Fluctuations in blood sugar levels can impact mood, attention, and behaviour. Diets that focus on complex carbohydrates, fibre, and protein can help stabilize blood sugar levels, reducing mood swings and improving focus.

4. **Food Sensitivities and Allergies**:

- Some individuals with ADHD or Autism may have sensitivities or allergies to certain foods. Identifying and eliminating trigger foods can lead to improvements in behaviour and overall well-being.

5. **Gut-Brain Connection**:

- There is a growing understanding of the gut-brain connection and its impact on mental health. Diets that support a healthy gut microbiome, such as those rich in fibre and fermented foods, may positively influence mood and cognitive function.

6. **Elimination of Artificial Additives**:

- Some studies suggest that artificial colours, flavours, and preservatives may exacerbate hyperactivity and impulsivity in individuals with ADHD. Eliminating or reducing these additives from the diet may be beneficial.

7. **Balanced Macronutrients**:

- A well-balanced diet that includes an appropriate mix of carbohydrates, proteins, and fats provides sustained energy and supports cognitive function. Diets that are too high in processed sugars or lacking in essential nutrients can negatively impact attention and behaviour.

8. **Individualized Approach**:

- It's important to recognize that individuals may respond differently to various dietary interventions. What works for one person may not work for another. Therefore, an individualized approach, possibly guided by a healthcare professional or nutritionist, is essential.

9. **Medication Complement:**

- For those on medication, a healthy diet can complement medical treatments. It may enhance the effectiveness of medications, reduce side effects, and contribute to overall well-being.

10. **Family Involvement**:

- In the case of children, involving the whole family in adopting a healthier diet can create a supportive environment and contribute to the success of dietary interventions.

Chapter 2: Breakfast Recipes

Nutrient-Packed Smoothie Bowl:

Ingredients:

- 1 cup frozen mixed berries (strawberries, blueberries, raspberries)
- 1 ripe banana, sliced
- 1/2 cup spinach leaves (fresh or frozen)
- 1/2 cup plain Greek yogurt
- 1/2 cup almond milk (or any milk of your choice)
- 1 tablespoon chia seeds
- 1 tablespoon honey or maple syrup (optional, for sweetness)
- Ice cubes (optional)

Toppings:

- Sliced fresh fruits (e.g., kiwi, berries, banana)
- Granola
- Nuts and seeds (e.g., almonds, chia seeds, pumpkin seeds)
- Coconut flakes
- Drizzle of nut butter (e.g., almond butter, peanut butter)

Instructions:

1. **Blend the Smoothie:**

- In a blender, combine the frozen mixed berries, sliced banana, spinach, Greek yoghurt, almond milk, chia seeds, and honey or maple syrup (if using).

- Blend until smooth and creamy. If the mixture is too thick, you can add more almond milk or water until you reach your desired consistency.

- Add ice cubes if you prefer a colder smoothie bowl.

2. **Pour into a Bowl:**

- Pour the smoothie into a bowl.

3. **Add Toppings**:

- Arrange the sliced fresh fruits, granola, nuts, seeds, and coconut flakes on top of the smoothie bowl in an aesthetically pleasing manner.

4. **Serve and Enjoy**:

- Serve the nutrient-packed smoothie bowl immediately.

- Use a spoon to mix the toppings with the smoothie as you eat.

Tips:

- Experiment with different fruits and vegetables based on personal preferences and nutritional needs.

- Adjust the sweetness by adding more or less honey or maple syrup.

- Feel free to customize the toppings based on what you have available or your favourite ingredients.

Quinoa Breakfast Porridge:

Ingredients:

- 1 cup quinoa, rinsed

- 2 cups almond milk (or any preferred milk)

- 1 teaspoon vanilla extract

- 1 tablespoon honey or maple syrup (adjust to taste)

- 1/2 teaspoon cinnamon

- Pinch of salt

- Fresh fruits (such as berries, and banana slices) for topping

- Nuts and seeds (optional, for added crunch)

Instructions:

1. **Rinse Quinoa**:

Rinse the quinoa under cold water to remove any bitterness.

2. **Cook Quinoa**: In a medium saucepan, combine the rinsed quinoa and almond milk. Bring to a boil, then reduce heat to low, cover, and simmer for about 15 minutes or until the quinoa is cooked and the liquid is absorbed.

3. **Sweeten and Flavor**: Once the quinoa is cooked, stir in the vanilla extract, honey (or maple syrup), cinnamon, and a pinch of salt. Adjust sweetness and flavour according to your taste preferences.

4. **Serve**: Spoon the quinoa porridge into bowls and top with fresh fruits, such as berries or banana slices.

5. **Optional Additions**: For added texture and flavour, consider sprinkling chopped nuts (like almonds or walnuts) and seeds (such as chia or flaxseeds) on top.

6. **Customization**: Feel free to customize the porridge with your favourite toppings, such as coconut flakes, shredded coconut, or a dollop of yoghurt.

Sweet Potato Hash with Eggs

Ingredients:

- 2 medium-sized sweet potatoes, peeled and diced into small cubes
    - 1 red bell pepper, diced
    - 1 yellow onion, finely chopped
    - 2 cloves garlic, minced
    - 2 tablespoons olive oil

- 1 teaspoon smoked paprika

- 1 teaspoon ground cumin

- Salt and pepper to taste

- 4 large eggs

- Fresh parsley or cilantro for garnish (optional)

Instructions:

1. **Prepare Vegetables**:

    - Peel and dice the sweet potatoes into small, uniform cubes.

    - Dice the red bell pepper and finely chop the yellow onion.

    - Mince the garlic cloves.

2. **Sauté Vegetables:**

    - In a large skillet, heat olive oil over medium heat.

    - Add the chopped onion and sauté until it becomes translucent.

    - Add the minced garlic and sauté for an additional 30 seconds.

    - Add the diced sweet potatoes and red bell pepper to the skillet.

    - Sprinkle smoked paprika, ground cumin, salt, and pepper over the vegetables.

    - Stir well to coat the vegetables evenly with the spices.

3. **Cook Sweet Potato Hash**:

    - Cover the skillet and let the sweet potatoes cook for about 15-20 minutes, or until they are tender. Stir occasionally to prevent sticking.

    - The hash is ready when the sweet potatoes are golden brown and cooked through.

4. **Prepare Eggs:**

- Create four wells in the sweet potato hash using a spoon.

- Crack an egg into each well.

5. **Cook Eggs:**

- Cover the skillet again and let the eggs cook until the whites are set, and the yolks are cooked to your preference. This typically takes about 5-7 minutes for a runny yolk.

6. **Serve:**

- Carefully scoop out portions of the sweet potato hash with an egg onto plates.

- Garnish with fresh parsley or cilantro if desired.

7. **Enjoy:**

- Serve the Sweet Potato Hash with Eggs hot, and enjoy a nutritious and delicious meal!

Oatmeal Pancakes with Berries:

Ingredients:

- 1 cup old-fashioned rolled oats
- 1 cup buttermilk (or a dairy-free alternative like almond milk)
- 1 large egg

- 2 tablespoons melted butter (or coconut oil for a dairy-free option)

- 2 tablespoons maple syrup or honey

- 1 teaspoon vanilla extract

- 1 cup all-purpose flour (or a gluten-free flour blend)

- 1 teaspoon baking powder

- 1/2 teaspoon baking soda

- 1/4 teaspoon salt

- 1 cup mixed berries (strawberries, blueberries, raspberries)

Instructions:

1. **Soak the Oats:**

- In a mixing bowl, combine the rolled oats and buttermilk. Allow them to soak for at least 15-20 minutes, or until the oats have absorbed most of the liquid.

2. **Prepare the Wet Ingredients**:

- After the oats have soaked, add the egg, melted butter (or coconut oil), maple syrup (or honey), and vanilla extract to the bowl. Mix well to combine.

3. **Combine Dry Ingredients:**

- In a separate bowl, whisk together the flour, baking powder, baking soda, and salt.

4. Combine Wet and Dry Ingredients:

- Add the dry ingredients to the wet ingredients and stir until just combined. Do not overmix; a few lumps are okay. The batter will be thick.

5. Fold in Berries:

- Gently fold the mixed berries into the pancake batter.

6. Preheat the Griddle or Pan:

- Preheat a griddle or non-stick pan over medium heat. If needed, lightly grease with butter or cooking spray.

7. Cook the Pancakes:

- Pour 1/4 cup portions of batter onto the griddle for each pancake. Spread the batter slightly with the back of a spoon to form a round shape.

8. Cook Until Bubbles Form:

- Cook until bubbles form on the surface of the pancakes, and the edges start to look set. This usually takes about 2-3 minutes.

9. Flip and Cook the Other Side:

- Carefully flip the pancakes with a spatula and cook for an additional 1-2 minutes on the other side, or until golden brown.

10. Serve:

- Remove the pancakes from the griddle and keep warm. Repeat the process with the remaining batter.

11. **Top and Enjoy:**

- Serve the pancakes warm, topped with additional berries and a drizzle of maple syrup or honey.

Chapter 3: Lunch Recipes

Grilled Chicken Salad with Avocado:

Ingredients:

- 1 lb boneless, skinless chicken breasts
- Salt and pepper to taste
- 2 tablespoons olive oil
- 1 teaspoon garlic powder
- 1 teaspoon paprika
- 1 teaspoon dried oregano
- Mixed salad greens (lettuce, spinach, arugula, etc.)
- Cherry tomatoes, halved
- Cucumber, sliced
- Red onion, thinly sliced
- 1 avocado, sliced
- Feta cheese, crumbled (optional)

For the Dressing:

- 3 tablespoons extra-virgin olive oil
- 2 tablespoons balsamic vinegar
- 1 teaspoon Dijon mustard
- Salt and pepper to taste

Instructions:

1. **Prepare the Chicken**:
   - Season the chicken breasts with salt, pepper, garlic powder, paprika, and dried oregano.
   - Drizzle olive oil over the chicken, ensuring it's evenly coated.
   - Preheat the grill or grill pan over medium-high heat.
   - Grill the chicken for about 6-8 minutes per side or until fully cooked.
   - Allow the chicken to rest for a few minutes before slicing it into strips.

2. **Make the Dressing**:
   - In a small bowl, whisk together the extra-virgin olive oil, balsamic vinegar, Dijon mustard, salt, and pepper. Adjust the seasoning to taste.

3. **Assemble the Salad**:
   - In a large salad bowl, combine the mixed salad greens, cherry tomatoes, cucumber slices, and red onion.

4. **Add Grilled Chicken**:
   - Place the sliced grilled chicken on top of the salad.

5. **Top with Avocado**:
   - Arrange the sliced avocado over the salad.

6. **Drizzle with Dressing**:

- Drizzle the prepared dressing over the salad. Toss gently to coat the salad ingredients evenly.

7. **Optional: Add Feta Cheese**:

- If desired, sprinkle crumbled feta cheese over the salad for an extra burst of flavour.

8. **Serve**:

- Divide the salad among plates and serve immediately.

Turkey and Veggie Wrap with Gluten-Free Tortilla:

Ingredients:

- Gluten-free tortillas (store-bought or homemade)
- Sliced turkey breast (nitrate-free for a healthier option)
- Hummus (homemade or your favourite store-bought variety)
- Mixed vegetables (e.g., bell peppers, cucumbers, carrots, spinach)
- Avocado, sliced
- Cherry tomatoes, halved

- Red onion, thinly sliced
- Olive oil
- Salt and pepper to taste

Instructions:

1. **Prepare the Vegetables**:
   - Wash and chop a variety of colourful vegetables like bell peppers, cucumbers, and carrots into thin strips.

2. **Sauté the Vegetables**:
   - In a pan, heat a bit of olive oil over medium heat.
   - Sauté the chopped vegetables until they are slightly tender but still have a crisp texture.
   - Season with salt and pepper to taste.

3. **Warm the Gluten-Free Tortillas**:
   - Warm the gluten-free tortillas according to the package instructions or heat them briefly on a dry skillet.

4. **Assemble the Wrap**:
   - Lay out the gluten-free tortillas on a clean surface or plate.
   - Spread a generous layer of hummus onto each tortilla, leaving space around the edges.

5. **Layer with Turkey and Vegetables**:
   - Place a few slices of nitrate-free turkey breast on top of the hummus layer.

- Add a portion of the sautéed vegetables evenly across the tortilla.

6. **Add Fresh Ingredients**:
    - Place slices of ripe avocado on the turkey and veggies.
    - Scatter halved cherry tomatoes and thinly sliced red onions for extra freshness.

7. **Fold and Roll:**
    - Carefully fold the sides of the tortilla over the filling.
    - Starting from one end, roll the tortilla tightly to create a wrap.

8. **Slice and Serve**:
    - Use a sharp knife to slice the wrap diagonally into halves or thirds.
    - Secure each slice with a toothpick if needed.

9. **Serve with Sides**:
    - Serve the Turkey and Veggie Wrap with additional hummus or a side salad for a complete meal.

Lentil and Vegetable Soup:

Ingredients:

- 1 cup dried green or brown lentils, rinsed and drained
- 1 onion, finely chopped
- 2 carrots, diced
- 2 celery stalks, chopped
- 3 cloves garlic, minced
- 1 can (14 oz) diced tomatoes, undrained
- 6 cups vegetable broth
- 1 teaspoon ground cumin
- 1 teaspoon ground coriander
- 1/2 teaspoon smoked paprika
- Salt and pepper to taste
- 2 cups chopped kale or spinach
- 2 tablespoons olive oil
- Fresh parsley for garnish (optional)

Instructions:

1. **Prepare the Lentils:**

   - Rinse the lentils under cold water and drain them. Set aside.

2. **Sauté Aromatics:**

   - In a large pot, heat olive oil over medium heat. Add chopped onion, carrots, and celery. Sauté until the vegetables are softened, about 5 minutes.

3. **Add Garlic and Spices**:

   - Add minced garlic to the pot and sauté for another minute until fragrant. Stir in ground cumin, ground coriander, smoked paprika, salt, and pepper.

4. **Combine Lentils and Tomatoes**:

   - Add the rinsed lentils and undrained diced tomatoes to the pot. Stir well to combine the ingredients.

5. **Pour in Vegetable Broth:**

   - Pour in the vegetable broth and bring the mixture to a boil. Reduce the heat to low, cover the pot, and let it simmer for about 25-30 minutes or until the lentils are tender.

6. **Add Greens**:

   - Stir in the chopped kale or spinach and cook for an additional 5 minutes until the greens are wilted.

7. **Adjust Seasoning**:

   - Taste the soup and adjust the seasoning with more salt and pepper if needed.

8. **Serve**:

   - Ladle the soup into bowls, garnish with fresh parsley if desired, and serve hot.

Quinoa and Chickpea Buddha Bowl:

Ingredients:
- 1 cup quinoa, rinsed
- 2 cups water or vegetable broth
- 1 can (15 oz) chickpeas, drained and rinsed
- 1 tablespoon olive oil
- 1 teaspoon ground cumin
- 1 teaspoon paprika
- Salt and pepper to taste

For the Bowl:
- 2 cups mixed greens (spinach, kale, or arugula)
- 1 cup cherry tomatoes, halved
- 1 cucumber, sliced
- 1 avocado, sliced
- 1/2 cup shredded carrots
- 1/4 cup red onion, thinly sliced

For the Dressing:
- 3 tablespoons olive oil
- 2 tablespoons balsamic vinegar
- 1 tablespoon Dijon mustard
- 1 clove garlic, minced
- Salt and pepper to taste

Instructions:

1. **Cook Quinoa:**
   - In a medium saucepan, combine quinoa and water or vegetable broth.
   - Bring to a boil, then reduce heat to low, cover, and simmer for 15-20 minutes or until quinoa is cooked and water is absorbed.
   - Fluff quinoa with a fork and set aside.

2. **Roast Chickpeas**:
   - Preheat the oven to 400°F (200°C).
   - In a bowl, toss chickpeas with olive oil, cumin, paprika, salt, and pepper.
   - Spread the chickpeas on a baking sheet and roast for 20-25 minutes or until crispy.

3. **Prepare Vegetables**:
   - Assemble the mixed greens, cherry tomatoes, cucumber, avocado, shredded carrots, and red onion in the Buddha Bowl.

4. **Make the Dressing:**
   - **In a small bowl**, whisk together olive oil, balsamic vinegar, Dijon mustard, minced garlic, salt, and pepper.

5. **Assemble the Buddha Bowl**:
   - Divide cooked quinoa, roasted chickpeas, and prepared vegetables among serving bowls.
   - Drizzle the dressing over the bowl.

6. **Enjoy**:

- Toss the ingredients together before eating, or enjoy the components   separately.

Chapter 4: Dinner Recipes

Baked Salmon with Lemon and Dill:

Ingredients:

- 4 salmon fillets
    - 2 tablespoons olive oil
    - 2 tablespoons fresh lemon juice
    - 2 cloves garlic, minced
    - 1 teaspoon dried dill (or 1 tablespoon fresh dill, chopped)
    - Salt and pepper to taste
    - Lemon slices for garnish
    - Fresh dill for garnish

Instructions:

1. **Preheat the Oven**:
    - Preheat your oven to 375°F (190°C).

2. **Prepare the Salmon**:
    - Pat the salmon fillets dry with paper towels. This helps the salmon to bake more evenly.

3. **Marinate the Salmon**:

- In a small bowl, whisk together the olive oil, lemon juice, minced garlic, dried dill (or fresh dill), salt, and pepper. This creates a flavorful marinade.

- Place the salmon fillets in a shallow dish and pour the marinade over them, ensuring each fillet is coated evenly. Let them marinate for at least 15-20 minutes, allowing the flavours to infuse.

4. **Bake the Salmon**:

- Line a baking sheet with parchment paper or lightly grease it.

- Transfer the marinated salmon fillets to the baking sheet.

- Bake in the preheated oven for 15-20 minutes, depending on the thickness of the fillets. The salmon is done when it easily flakes with a fork.

5. **Garnish and Serve**:

- Once the salmon is baked, remove it from the oven.

- Garnish with fresh dill and lemon slices for a burst of freshness.

- Serve the baked salmon hot, accompanied by your favourite side dishes like steamed vegetables, quinoa, or a green salad.

6. **Optional: Lemon Butter Sauce (Optional):**

- For an extra touch, you can prepare a simple lemon butter sauce by melting 2 tablespoons of butter in a small saucepan and adding a splash of lemon juice. Drizzle this sauce over the baked salmon just before serving.

Spaghetti Squash with Tomato Basil Sauce:

Ingredients:

- 1 medium-sized spaghetti squash
- 2 tablespoons olive oil
- 2 cloves garlic, minced
- 1 can (about 14 oz) crushed tomatoes
- 1 teaspoon dried oregano
- 1 teaspoon dried basil
- Salt and pepper to taste
- Fresh basil leaves for garnish
- Grated Parmesan cheese (optional)

Instructions:

1. **Prepare the Spaghetti Squash**:
   - Preheat your oven to 400°F (200°C).
   - Cut the spaghetti squash in half lengthwise and scoop out the seeds.
   - Drizzle the cut sides with olive oil, and season with salt and pepper.
   - Place the squash halves, cut side down, on a baking sheet.
   - Bake for 40-50 minutes or until the squash is tender and the strands can be easily pulled away with a fork.

2. **Make the Tomato Basil Sauce**:

- In a saucepan, heat 2 tablespoons of olive oil over medium heat.

- Add minced garlic and sauté until it becomes fragrant, about 1 minute.

- Pour in the crushed tomatoes, dried oregano, dried basil, salt, and pepper.

- Bring the sauce to a simmer and let it cook for 15-20 minutes, allowing the flavours to meld.

- Adjust salt and pepper to taste.

3. **Prepare the Dish:**

- Once the spaghetti squash is cooked, use a fork to scrape the flesh into "spaghetti" strands.

- Place the spaghetti squash on a plate or in a bowl.

- Top the spaghetti squash with the tomato basil sauce.

4. **Garnish and Serve**:

- Garnish with fresh basil leaves and, if desired, sprinkle with grated Parmesan cheese.

- Serve warm and enjoy!

Stir-fried tofu with Broccoli and Brown Rice:

Ingredients:

- 1 cup brown rice, cooked
- 1 block of firm tofu, pressed and cubed
- 2 cups broccoli florets
- 1 red bell pepper, thinly sliced
- 1 carrot, julienned
- 3 tablespoons soy sauce (or tamari for a gluten-free option)
- 2 tablespoons sesame oil
- 2 cloves garlic, minced
- 1 tablespoon fresh ginger, grated
- 2 tablespoons rice vinegar
- 1 tablespoon maple syrup or agave nectar
- 2 green onions, chopped
- Sesame seeds for garnish (optional)
- Salt and pepper to taste

Instructions:

1. **Prepare Brown Rice**:

   - Cook the brown rice according to package instructions. Set aside.

2. **Press and Prepare Tofu**:

   - Press the tofu to remove excess water. Cut it into cubes.

3. **Stir-Fry Tofu**:

   - Heat 1 tablespoon of sesame oil in a large wok or skillet over medium-high heat.

- Add the cubed tofu and stir-fry until golden brown on all sides, about 5-7 minutes.

- Once cooked, remove tofu from the pan and set aside.

4. **Prepare Vegetables**:

- In the same pan, add another tablespoon of sesame oil.

- Add minced garlic and grated ginger, and sauté for about 1 minute until fragrant.

- Add broccoli, red bell pepper, and julienned carrot to the pan. Stir-fry for 3-5 minutes until the vegetables are slightly tender but still crisp.

5. **Combine Tofu and Vegetables**:

- Return the cooked tofu to the pan with the vegetables. Mix well.

6. **Prepare Sauce:**

- In a small bowl, whisk together soy sauce, rice vinegar, and maple syrup or agave nectar.

- Pour the sauce over the tofu and vegetables. Toss to coat evenly.

7. **Finish and Serve:**

- Add the cooked brown rice to the stir-fried tofu and vegetables. Stir everything together until well combined.

- Season with salt and pepper to taste.

- Garnish with chopped green onions and sesame seeds if desired.

8. **Serve Warm**:

- Divide the stir-fried tofu, vegetables, and brown rice among serving plates.

- Enjoy this nutritious and delicious meal warm.

Turkey and Sweet Potato Casserole:

Ingredients:
- 1 lb ground turkey
- 2 large sweet potatoes, peeled and diced
- 1 onion, finely chopped
- 2 cloves garlic, minced
- 1 cup spinach, chopped
- 1 can (14 oz) diced tomatoes, drained
- 1 teaspoon dried thyme
- 1 teaspoon dried oregano
- Salt and pepper to taste
- Olive oil for cooking
- 1 cup shredded mozzarella cheese (optional)

Instructions:

1. **Preheat the Oven**:

   - Preheat your oven to 375°F (190°C).

2. **Cook the Sweet Potatoes:**

   - Boil or steam the sweet potato chunks until they are fork-tender. Drain and set aside.

3. **Sauté Onion and Garlic:**

   - In a large skillet, heat olive oil over medium heat. Add chopped onions and minced garlic, and sauté until softened.

4. **Brown the Turkey:**

   - Add the ground turkey to the skillet and cook until browned. Season with thyme, oregano, salt, and pepper.

5. **Combine Ingredients:**

   - In a large mixing bowl, combine the cooked sweet potatoes, turkey mixture, chopped spinach, and diced tomatoes. Mix well.

6. **Assemble the Casserole:**

   - Transfer the mixture to a baking dish. If desired, sprinkle shredded mozzarella cheese on top.

7. **Bake**:

   - Bake in the preheated oven for about 25-30 minutes or until the top is golden brown, and the casserole is heated through.

8. Serve:

- Allow the casserole to cool slightly before serving. Garnish with fresh herbs if desired.

Chapter 5: Snack Recipes

Veggie Sticks with Hummus:

Ingredients:

- Carrot sticks
    - Cucumber sticks
    - Bell pepper strips (assorted colours)
    - Cherry tomatoes, halved
    - Celery sticks
    - Hummus (store-bought or homemade)

For Hummus:

- 1 can (15 ounces) chickpeas, drained and rinsed
    - 1/4 cup tahini
    - 1/4 cup extra virgin olive oil
    - 1 clove garlic, minced
    - 1 teaspoon ground cumin
    - 1/2 teaspoon paprika
    - 2 tablespoons lemon juice
    - Salt and pepper to taste
    - Water (as needed for desired consistency)

Instructions:

1. **Prepare the Hummus**:

a. In a food processor, combine chickpeas, tahini, olive oil, minced garlic, ground cumin, paprika, and lemon juice.

b. Blend until smooth, scraping down the sides as needed. If the hummus is too thick, you can add water, one tablespoon at a time, until you achieve the desired consistency.

c. Season with salt and pepper to taste. Adjust the seasonings as needed.

2. **Prepare the Veggie Sticks:**

a. Wash and peel (if necessary) the carrots and cucumber. Cut them into sticks.

b. Wash and cut the bell peppers into thin strips.

c. Cut celery into sticks.

d. Halve cherry tomatoes.

3. **Assemble**:

a. Arrange the veggie sticks on a serving platter.

b. Place a bowl of homemade or store-bought hummus in the centre of the platter.

c. Optionally, drizzle a bit of extra virgin olive oil over the hummus and sprinkle with a pinch of paprika for garnish.

4. **Serve**:

a. Serve immediately and enjoy the Veggie Sticks with Hummus as a snack or appetizer.

Trail Mix with Nuts and Dried Fruits:

Ingredients:
- 1 cup almonds
- 1 cup walnuts
- 1 cup cashews
- 1 cup pumpkin seeds
- 1 cup dried cranberries
- 1 cup dried apricots, chopped
- 1 cup dark chocolate chips (optional)

Instructions:

1. **Select Your Nuts**:

- Choose a variety of nuts based on your preferences. Almonds, walnuts, cashews, and pumpkin seeds are excellent choices.

2. **Roast Nuts (Optional):**

- If desired, you can roast the nuts for added flavour. Spread them on a baking sheet and roast in the oven at 350°F (180°C) for about 10 minutes or until they are lightly golden. Allow them to cool completely.

3. **Prepare Dried Fruits:**

- Chop dried apricots into bite-sized pieces. If your dried cranberries are large, you can also chop them for a more even distribution in the mix.

4. **Combine Ingredients:**

- In a large bowl, mix the roasted nuts, dried cranberries, chopped apricots, and pumpkin seeds. If you have any other favourite nuts or seeds, feel free to add them.

5. **Add Chocolate (Optional):**

- For a touch of sweetness, you can include dark chocolate chips. Make sure to choose a variety with a high cocoa content for added health benefits.

6. **Mix Thoroughly:**

- Gently toss all the ingredients until they are well combined. Ensure an even distribution of nuts, seeds, fruits, and chocolate throughout the mix.

7. **Store in an Airtight Container:**

- Transfer the trail mix to an airtight container to keep it fresh. It can be stored at room temperature for several weeks.

Variations:

- Protein-Packed Mix:

- Add roasted chickpeas or edamame for an extra protein boost.

- Tropical Twist:

- Use dried pineapple and mango along with macadamia nuts for a tropical flavour.

- Spicy Kick:

- Sprinkle the mix with a pinch of cayenne pepper or chilli powder for a spicy trail mix.

- Nut-Free Version:

- Replace nuts with roasted seeds such as sunflower seeds and pepitas for a nut-free alternative.

Baked Kale Chips:

Ingredients:

- 1 bunch of fresh kale

- 1-2 tablespoons olive oil

- Salt and pepper to taste

- Optional: Parmesan cheese, nutritional yeast, garlic powder, or other seasonings of your choice

Instructions:

1. Preheat the Oven:

- Preheat your oven to 350°F (175°C).

2. Prepare the Kale:

- Wash the kale leaves thoroughly and pat them dry with a paper towel. Remove the tough stems, and tear the leaves into bite-sized pieces.

3. Massage with Olive Oil:

- In a large bowl, drizzle the torn kale leaves with olive oil. Using your hands, massage the oil into the kale leaves, ensuring that each piece is well-coated. Massaging helps to soften the kale and make it more enjoyable.

4. **Seasoning**:

- Sprinkle salt and pepper over the kale. You can also add additional seasonings such as garlic powder, Parmesan cheese, nutritional yeast, or any other flavours you prefer. Toss the kale in the bowl to evenly distribute the seasonings.

5. **Arrange on Baking Sheet**:

- Line a baking sheet with parchment paper or use a silicone baking mat. Spread the kale leaves in a single layer, making sure they are not overcrowded. This allows them to crisp up in the oven.

6. **Bake**:

- Place the baking sheet in the preheated oven and bake for approximately 10-15 minutes, or until the edges of the kale are crispy and slightly browned. Keep a close eye on them to prevent burning.

7. **Cool and Enjoy:**

- Remove the kale chips from the oven and let them cool on the baking sheet for a few minutes. The kale chips will continue to crisp up as they cool. Once cooled, transfer them to a serving bowl.

8. **Serve**:

- Enjoy your Baked Kale Chips as a healthy snack on their own, or pair them with your favourite dip.

Tips:

- Experiment with different seasonings to find your favourite flavour combination.

- Ensure the kale leaves are thoroughly dry before massaging with oil to achieve maximum crispiness.

- Store any leftover kale chips in an airtight container to maintain their crispiness.

Yogurt Parfait with Fresh Berries:

Ingredients:

- 1 cup plain Greek yoghurt (or your preferred yoghurt)

- 1 cup mixed fresh berries (such as strawberries, blueberries, raspberries)

- 1/4 cup granola (choose a variety without added sugars if possible)

- 2 tablespoons honey or maple syrup (optional, for sweetness)

- 1/4 cup chopped nuts (e.g., almonds, walnuts) for crunch (optional)

- 1 teaspoon chia seeds for added nutrition (optional)

- Fresh mint leaves for garnish (optional)

Instructions:

1. **Prepare the Yogurt:**

- In a bowl, scoop out the Greek yoghurt. If you're using regular yoghurt, you might want to strain it to achieve a thicker consistency.

2. **Layering**:

- In a glass or a bowl, start by adding a layer of Greek yoghurt at the bottom.

- Add a layer of mixed fresh berries on top of the yoghurt.

- Sprinkle a layer of granola over the berries. This adds crunch and additional fibre.

- Optionally, drizzle honey or maple syrup over the granola for sweetness.

- Repeat the layering process until you reach the top of the glass or bowl.

3. **Top it Off:**

- Finish by topping the parfait with a final layer of fresh berries.

- Add a sprinkle of chopped nuts for extra texture and healthy fats.

- If desired, sprinkle chia seeds for added nutritional benefits.

4. **Garnish**:

- Garnish with fresh mint leaves for a burst of freshness and a visually appealing touch.

5. **Serve**:

- Serve immediately to enjoy the crispness of the granola or refrigerate for a short time if you prefer a slightly chilled parfait.

Chapter 6: Beverages

Green Smoothie with Spinach and Pineapple:

Ingredients:

- 1 cup fresh spinach leaves, washed

    - 1 cup pineapple chunks (fresh or frozen)

    - 1 ripe banana

    - 1/2 cup Greek yoghurt (or dairy-free alternative for a vegan option)

    - 1/2 cup coconut water or plain water

    - Ice cubes (optional)

    - Honey or agave syrup (optional, for sweetness)

Instructions:

1. **Prepare the Ingredients**:
    - Wash the fresh spinach leaves thoroughly.
    - If using fresh pineapple, peel and chop it into chunks. If using frozen pineapple, no need to thaw.
    - Peel the ripe banana.

2. **Blend the Greens**:

   - In a blender, add the fresh spinach leaves.

3. **Add Fruits**:

   - Add the pineapple chunks and the peeled banana to the blender.

4. **Include the Liquid**:

   - Pour in the coconut water or plain water.

5. **Add Creaminess**:

   - Spoon in the Greek yoghurt or dairy-free alternative.

6. **Optional Sweetener:**

   - **If you prefer a** sweeter taste, add honey or agave syrup to taste.

7. **Blend Until Smooth:**

   - Secure the lid on the blender and blend all the ingredients until smooth. If the smoothie is too thick, you can add more liquid.

8. **Adjust Consistency**:

   - If desired, add ice cubes and blend again until the smoothie reaches your preferred consistency.

9. **Taste and Adjust**:

   - Taste the smoothie and adjust the sweetness or thickness by adding more sweetener or liquid if needed.

10. **Serve**:

   - Pour the green smoothie into glasses and serve immediately.

Optional Add-ins:

   - Chia seeds or flaxseeds for added nutrition and texture.

   - Protein powder for an extra protein boost.

   - A handful of mint leaves for a refreshing twist.

Herbal Tea Infusions:

Recipes:

1. **Chamomile and Lavender Bliss:**
   - **Ingredients:**
   - 1 tablespoon dried chamomile flowers
   - 1 teaspoon dried lavender buds
   - Instructions:
   1. Combine chamomile flowers and lavender buds in a teapot.
   2. Pour hot water over the herbs and let steep for 5-7 minutes.
   3. Strain and enjoy this calming infusion before bedtime.

2. **Peppermint and Lemon Zest Refresher:**
   - **Ingredients:**
   - 1 tablespoon dried peppermint leaves

- 1 teaspoon lemon zest

- Instructions:

1. Place peppermint leaves and lemon zest in a teapot.

2. Pour hot water over the herbs and let steep for 5-7 minutes.

3. Strain and enjoy this refreshing infusion, perfect for an afternoon pick-me-up.

3. **Ginger and Turmeric Wellness Tea**:

- **Ingredients**:

- 1 tablespoon grated fresh ginger

- 1 teaspoon ground turmeric

- Instructions:

1. Combine grated ginger and turmeric in a teapot.

2. Pour hot water over the herbs and let steep for 7-10 minutes.

3. Strain and savour the anti-inflammatory benefits of this immune-boosting infusion.

4. **Rosehip and Hibiscus Beauty Elixir:**

- **Ingredients:**

- 2 tablespoons dried rosehip

- 1 tablespoon dried hibiscus petals

- Instructions:

1. Place rosehip and hibiscus petals in a teapot.

2. Pour hot water over the herbs and let steep for 5-7 minutes.

3. Strain and enjoy this vibrant infusion rich in antioxidants.

5. **Nettle and Raspberry Leaf Nourisher:**

- **Ingredients:**

- 1 tablespoon dried nettle leaves

- 1 tablespoon dried raspberry leaves

- Instructions:

1. Combine nettle leaves and raspberry leaves in a teapot.

2. Pour hot water over the herbs and let steep for 7-10 minutes.

3. Strain and sip on this nutrient-rich infusion for overall well-being.

Coconut Water with Chia Seeds:

Ingredients:

- 2 cups coconut water

- 2 tablespoons chia seeds

- 1 tablespoon honey or maple syrup (optional)

- Sliced fruits (such as strawberries, kiwi, or pineapple) for garnish (optional)

- Ice cubes (optional)

Instructions:

1. **Prepare the Chia Seeds**:

- In a bowl, combine chia seeds with 1/2 cup of coconut water.

- Stir well to ensure that the chia seeds are evenly distributed.

2. **Soak the Chia Seeds**:

- Let the chia seeds soak in the coconut water for at least 15-20 minutes, or until they develop a gel-like consistency.

- Stir the mixture a few times during this period to prevent clumping.

3. **Combine with Coconut Water**:

- After the chia seeds have absorbed the liquid and formed a gel, mix them into the remaining coconut water.

- If desired, add honey or maple syrup for sweetness. Adjust the sweetness according to your taste preferences.

4. **Chill and Serve:**

- Refrigerate the coconut water with chia seeds for an additional 1-2 hours to allow it to cool and enhance the flavours.

- Before serving, stir the mixture again to ensure the chia seeds are evenly distributed.

5. **Garnish and Enjoy:**

- Serve the coconut water with chia seeds over ice cubes, if desired.

- Garnish with sliced fruits for added freshness and flavour.

Freshly Squeezed Orange Juice:

Ingredients:

- 4-6 large, ripe oranges

Instructions:

1. **Select and Prep the Oranges**:
   - Choose fresh and ripe oranges for the best flavour. They should feel heavy for their size and have a bright, vibrant colour.
   - Wash the oranges thoroughly under running water.

2. **Cut and Juice:**
   - Cut each orange in half.
   - Using a citrus juicer or a manual juicing tool, squeeze the juice from each orange half. You can also use an electric juicer for larger quantities.

3. **Strain (Optional):**
   - If you prefer a smoother juice without pulp, you can strain the freshly squeezed juice using a fine-mesh strainer or cheesecloth.

4. **Serve**:
   - Pour the freshly squeezed orange juice into a glass.
   - Add ice cubes if desired, or refrigerate the juice before serving for a chilled experience.

5. Garnish (Optional):

- Garnish with a slice of orange on the rim of the glass for a decorative touch.

Variations:

1. Orange-Ginger Zest:

- Add a teaspoon of freshly grated ginger to the orange juice for a zesty and slightly spicy kick.

2. Minty Citrus Splash:

- Mix in a handful of fresh mint leaves or muddle them at the bottom of the glass for a minty twist.

3. Sparkling Citrus Refresher:

- Combine freshly squeezed orange juice with sparkling water for a fizzy, refreshing beverage.

4. Citrus Berry Blend:

- Mix in other citrus fruits like grapefruit or tangerine, and add a handful of mixed berries for a colourful and flavorful blend.

5. Turmeric Citrus Elixir:

- Stir in a pinch of turmeric powder for an added anti-inflammatory boost.

6. **Coconut Orange Fusion**:

- Mix equal parts of freshly squeezed orange juice and coconut water for a tropical and hydrating drink.

52

Chapter 7: Special Treats

Avocado Chocolate Mousse:

Ingredients:

- 2 ripe avocados, peeled and pitted
- 1/4 cup cocoa powder (unsweetened)
- 1/4 cup maple syrup or honey (adjust to taste)
- 1/4 cup almond milk (or any preferred milk)
- 1 teaspoon vanilla extract
- A pinch of salt
- Optional toppings: shaved chocolate, berries, or chopped nuts

Instructions:

1. **Prepare Avocados**:

   - Scoop out the flesh of the ripe avocados and place them in a blender or food processor.

2. **Blend Avocados**:

   - Blend the avocados until they become smooth and creamy.

3. Add Cocoa Powder:

   - Add cocoa powder to the blended avocados. Make sure to use unsweetened cocoa powder for a healthier option.

4. Sweeten It Up:

   - Add maple syrup or honey to sweeten the mousse. Adjust the sweetness according to your taste preferences.

5. Pour in Milk:

   - Pour in the almond milk (or your preferred milk) to help achieve the desired consistency and enhance creaminess.

6. Add Vanilla and Salt:

   - Add vanilla extract and a pinch of salt to enhance the flavour. The salt can bring out the richness of the chocolate.

7. Blend Again:

   - Blend all the ingredients until the mixture is smooth and well combined. You may need to stop and scrape down the sides to ensure everything is mixed evenly.

8. Chill:

   - Transfer the chocolate avocado mixture to individual serving bowls or glasses and refrigerate for at least 1-2 hours to chill and set.

9. **Serve**:

   - Once chilled, you can serve the avocado chocolate mousse as is or add your favourite toppings such as shaved chocolate, berries, or chopped nuts.

Banana and Almond Butter Bites:

Ingredients:

- 2 large bananas, ripe
    - 1/2 cup almond butter (unsweetened)
    - 1/4 cup shredded coconut (unsweetened)
    - 1/4 cup chopped almonds
    - 1 teaspoon cinnamon
    - Dark chocolate chips (optional, for drizzling)

Instructions:

1. **Prepare the Ingredients**:
   - Peel and slice the bananas into bite-sized rounds.
   - In a small bowl, mix the almond butter until it's smooth and easy to spread.

2. Assemble the Bites:

- Take a banana slice and spread a thin layer of almond butter on top.

3. Add Toppings:

- **Sprinkle** shredded coconut and chopped almonds on the almond butter.

4. Sprinkle with Cinnamon:

- Dust the bites with a pinch of cinnamon for added flavour.

5. Optional Chocolate Drizzle:

- If you have dark chocolate chips, melt them in the microwave or using a double boiler. Drizzle the melted chocolate over the banana bites for an extra indulgent touch.

6. Set and Serve:

- Place the banana and almond butter bites on a plate or tray.
- If you've added chocolate, allow it to set by placing the bites in the refrigerator for about 10-15 minutes.

7. Serve and Enjoy:

- Once set, these bites are ready to be enjoyed! They make for a delightful snack or a healthy dessert.

Notes:

- **Variations**: Feel free to get creative with toppings. You can add a sprinkle of chia seeds, crushed pistachios, or even a drizzle of honey for different flavours.

- **Storage**: These bites are best enjoyed fresh, but you can store them in an airtight container in the refrigerator for a day or two.

- **Allergen Information**: Ensure that the almond butter is free from any allergens that may affect those for whom you are preparing these bites. Consider using sunflower seed butter as an alternative if there are nut allergies.

Gluten-Free Chocolate Chip Cookies:

Ingredients:
- 1 cup gluten-free all-purpose flour
- 1/2 teaspoon baking soda
- 1/4 teaspoon salt
- 1/2 cup unsalted butter, softened
- 1/2 cup brown sugar, packed
- 1/4 cup granulated sugar
- 1 large egg
- 1 teaspoon vanilla extract
- 1 cup gluten-free chocolate chips

Instructions:

1. **Preheat the Oven:**
   - **Preheat your** oven to 350°F (175°C).

2. **Prepare Baking Sheet**:
   - Line a baking sheet with parchment paper to prevent the cookies from sticking.

3. **Mix Dry Ingredients**:
   - In a bowl, whisk together the gluten-free all-purpose flour, baking soda, and salt. Set aside.

4. **Cream Butter and Sugar**s:
   - In a separate large mixing bowl, cream together the softened butter, brown sugar, and granulated sugar until light and fluffy.

5. **Add Egg and Vanilla:**
   - Add the egg and vanilla extract to the butter-sugar mixture. Mix until well combined.

6. **Combine Wet and Dry Ingredients**:
   - Gradually add the dry ingredients to the wet ingredients, mixing just until combined. Be careful not to overmix.

7. Fold in Chocolate Chips:

- Gently fold in the gluten-free chocolate chips until evenly distributed throughout the cookie dough.

8. Scoop Cookie Dough:

- Use a cookie scoop or a tablespoon to drop rounded portions of dough onto the prepared baking sheet, leaving enough space between each cookie.

9. Bake:

- Bake in the preheated oven for 10-12 minutes or until the edges are lightly golden. The centre may still appear slightly soft, but they will firm up as they cool.

10. Cool:

- Allow the cookies to cool on the baking sheet for a few minutes before transferring them to a wire rack to cool completely.

11. Enjoy:

- Once completely cooled, enjoy your delicious gluten-free chocolate chip cookies!

Note:

- It's important to use a gluten-free all-purpose flour blend that is suitable for baking cookies. You can find pre-made blends in many grocery stores.

- Ensure that all your ingredients, including the chocolate chips, are labelled gluten-free to avoid cross-contamination.

Berry Sorbet with Mint:

Ingredients:

- 2 cups mixed berries (strawberries, blueberries, raspberries, blackberries)
- 1/2 cup fresh mint leaves, loosely packed
- 1/4 cup honey or maple syrup (adjust according to taste)
- 1 tablespoon freshly squeezed lemon juice
- 1/2 cup cold water

Instructions:

1. **Prepare the Berries**:
   - Rinse the berries under cold water and remove any stems.
   - If using strawberries, hull and slice them.

2. **Blending**:
   - In a blender or food processor, combine the mixed berries, fresh mint leaves, honey or maple syrup, and lemon juice.
   - Blend until you achieve a smooth puree.

3. **Strain (Optional)**:

   - If you prefer a smoother sorbet, you can strain the mixture using a fine-mesh sieve to remove seeds and any larger pieces.

4. **Add Water**:

   - Add cold water to the berry puree and blend briefly to combine. The water helps achieve a smoother texture.

5. **Taste and Adjust**:

   - Taste the mixture and adjust the sweetness by adding more honey or maple syrup if needed.

6. **Chill**:

   - Pour the sorbet mixture into a shallow dish or a bowl.
   - Cover and place it in the refrigerator to chill for at least 2 hours.

7. **Freeze**:

   - Once the sorbet mixture is chilled, transfer it to an ice cream maker.
   - Follow the manufacturer's instructions to churn the sorbet until it reaches a slushy, frozen consistency.

8. **Serve**:

   - Transfer the churned sorbet to a lidded container and freeze for an additional 2 hours or until firm.
   - Scoop the berry sorbet into bowls or cones.

9. **Garnish**:

   - Garnish the sorbet with additional fresh mint leaves for a burst of flavour.

10. **Enjoy**:

   - Serve immediately and enjoy the refreshing and naturally sweet taste of the berry sorbet with a hint of mint.

Chapter 8: Desserts

Almond Flour Brownies:

Ingredients:

- 1 cup almond flour
    - 1/2 cup unsweetened cocoa powder
    - 1/2 teaspoon baking powder
    - 1/4 teaspoon salt
    - 1/2 cup unsalted butter, melted
    - 1 cup granulated sugar or a sugar substitute (like erythritol for a low-carb option)
    - 3 large eggs
    - 1 teaspoon vanilla extract
    - 1/2 cup chocolate chips (optional)
    - Chopped nuts (optional)

Instructions:

1. **Preheat the Oven:**
    - Preheat your oven to 350°F (175°C).

2. **Prepare the Pan**:

- Grease a square baking pan or line it with parchment paper for easy removal.

3. **Mix Dry Ingredients**:

- In a medium-sized bowl, whisk together the almond flour, cocoa powder, baking powder, and salt. Set aside.

4. **Combine Wet Ingredients**:

- In another bowl, mix the melted butter and sugar until well combined. Add the eggs one at a time, beating well after each addition. Stir in the vanilla extract.

5. **Combine Dry and Wet Mixtures**:

- Gradually add the dry ingredients to the wet ingredients, stirring until just combined. Be careful not to overmix.

6. **Add Chocolate Chips (Optional)**:

- If you want extra chocolatey goodness, fold in chocolate chips or chunks into the batter.

7. **Transfer to Pan:**

- Pour the batter into the prepared baking pan, spreading it evenly.

8. **Bake**:

- Bake in the preheated oven for 25-30 minutes, or until a toothpick inserted into the centre comes out with moist crumbs (not wet batter).

9. **Cool**:

- Allow the brownies to cool in the pan for about 10-15 minutes before transferring them to a wire rack to cool completely.

10. **Slice and Serve**:

- Once completely cooled, slice the brownies into squares or rectangles. If desired, sprinkle with chopped nuts.

11. **Enjoy**:

- Serve and enjoy these delicious almond flour brownies!

Coconut Flour Lemon Bars:

Ingredients:

For the Crust:

- 1 cup coconut flour
- 1/2 cup melted coconut oil
- 1/4 cup honey or maple syrup

- A pinch of salt

For the Lemon Filling:
- 4 large eggs
- 1 cup fresh lemon juice (about 4-6 lemons)
- Zest of 2 lemons
- 1/2 cup honey or maple syrup
- 1/4 cup coconut flour
- 1/2 teaspoon baking powder

Instructions:

1. **Preheat the Oven**:

- Preheat your oven to 350°F (175°C). Grease a baking dish (usually 8x8 inches) or line it with parchment paper for easy removal.

2. **Make the Crust:**

- In a bowl, combine the coconut flour, melted coconut oil, honey or maple syrup, and a pinch of salt.
- Mix until a dough forms.
- Press the dough evenly into the bottom of the prepared baking dish to create the crust.

3. **Bake the Crust**:

- Bake the crust in the preheated oven for about 10-12 minutes or until it's lightly golden. Remove from the oven and let it cool while you prepare the filling.

4. Prepare the Lemon Filling:

- In a separate bowl, whisk together the eggs, fresh lemon juice, lemon zest, honey or maple syrup, coconut flour, and baking powder.

- Ensure that there are no lumps in the mixture.

5. Pour Filling over the Crust:

- Pour the lemon filling over the cooled coconut flour crust, spreading it evenly.

6. Bake Again:

- Bake in the oven for 20-25 minutes or until the edges are set, and the centre is slightly firm.

7. Cool and Refrigerate:

- Allow the lemon bars to cool completely in the baking dish. Once cooled, refrigerate for at least 2 hours or until the bars are well-chilled.

8. Cut into Bars:

- Once chilled, lift the bars out of the baking dish using the parchment paper, if used.

- Cut into squares or bars.

9. Serve:

- Serve the Coconut Flour Lemon Bars chilled. Optionally, dust with powdered sugar or sprinkle with shredded coconut for garnish.

Chia Seed Pudding with Mixed Berries:

Ingredients:

- 1/4 cup chia seeds

- 1 cup almond milk (or any preferred milk)

- 1-2 tablespoons maple syrup or honey (adjust to taste)

- 1/2 teaspoon vanilla extract

- Mixed berries (strawberries, blueberries, raspberries) for topping

- Nuts or seeds for added crunch (optional)

Instructions:

1. **Mix the Chia Seeds and Liquid**:

- In a bowl, combine chia seeds and almond milk. Stir well to make sure the chia seeds are evenly distributed.

2. **Sweeten and Flavor:**

- Add maple syrup or honey to sweeten the mixture. Adjust the sweetness according to your taste preference.

- Stir in the vanilla extract for flavour. Mix thoroughly.

3. **Refrigerate Overnight**:

- Cover the bowl and refrigerate the mixture for at least 4 hours or overnight. The chia seeds will absorb the liquid and create a pudding-like consistency.

4. **Stir Occasionally**:

- After the first hour, stir the mixture again to prevent clumping. This ensures a smooth and consistent texture.

5. **Serve and Top**:

- Once the chia pudding has set, give it a final stir. Spoon it into serving bowls or jars.

- Top the pudding with a generous amount of mixed berries. You can also add nuts or seeds for an extra crunch and nutritional boost.

6. **Enjoy**:

- Serve chilled and enjoy a healthy and satisfying chia seed pudding with the goodness of mixed berries.

Tips and Variations:

- Experiment with different types of milk like coconut milk, soy milk, or cow's milk based on dietary preferences.

- Customize the sweetness by adjusting the amount of maple syrup or honey.

- Add a pinch of cinnamon or nutmeg for extra flavour.

- Include other toppings like shredded coconut, granola, or sliced bananas.

Apple Cinnamon Baked Oatmeal:

Ingredients:

- 2 cups old-fashioned rolled oats
- 1 teaspoon baking powder
- 1/2 teaspoon cinnamon
- 1/4 teaspoon salt
- 1 1/2 cups almond milk (or any preferred milk)
- 1/4 cup maple syrup or honey
- 2 tablespoons melted coconut oil or butter
- 1 large egg, beaten
- 1 teaspoon vanilla extract
- 2 medium-sized apples, peeled, cored, and diced
- 1/3 cup chopped nuts (walnuts or pecans), optional
- Additional cinnamon for sprinkling on top
- Fresh berries or yoghurt for serving (optional)

Instructions:

1. **Preheat the Oven**:

Preheat your oven to 350°F (175°C). Grease a baking dish with coconut oil or cooking spray.

2. **Mix Dry Ingredients**:

In a large mixing bowl, combine the rolled oats, baking powder, cinnamon, and salt. Mix well to ensure even distribution of the ingredients.

3. **Combine Wet Ingredients**:

In another bowl, whisk together the almond milk, maple syrup or honey, melted coconut oil or butter, beaten egg, and vanilla extract.

4. **Combine Wet and Dry Mixtures**:

Pour the wet ingredients into the bowl with the dry ingredients. Stir until well combined.

5. **Add Apples and Nuts**:

Gently fold in the diced apples and chopped nuts (if using). The apples will add sweetness and a delightful texture to the baked oatmeal.

6. **Transfer to Baking Dish**:

Pour the oatmeal mixture into the greased baking dish, spreading it evenly.

7. **Bake**:

Place the baking dish in the preheated oven and bake for about 30-35 minutes or until the edges are golden brown, and the centre is set.

8. **Cool and Serve:**

Allow the baked oatmeal to cool for a few minutes before slicing it into squares or scooping it out. Serve warm, and if desired, top with a sprinkle of cinnamon, fresh berries, or a dollop of yoghurt.

Conclusion

As we come to the end of our culinary adventure through the "ADHD & Autism Diet Cookbook," we ask you to relish the tremendous influence that mindful eating can have on the delicate fabric of health and well-being. This cookbook offers a portal to a transformational approach to eating that goes well beyond the kitchen.

Each dish is proof that the link between nutrition and neurological well-being is more than just a theory; it's a physical fact. You're not only creating meals when you embrace the vivid, nutrient-rich ingredients expertly picked for these recipes; you're also creating an environment that promotes attention, energy, and emotional balance.

You possess a compass directing you towards a more lively and harmonious existence in your hands, not simply a collection of recipes. Each person's path to wellness is unique, and this cookbook acts as an adaptable companion, adjusting to a wide range of tastes, preferences, and dietary requirements.

As you explore the tempting tastes and inventive combinations contained herein, keep in mind that this is more than a cookbook— it's an invitation to an intentional living, where every mouthful is a step towards a brighter, more balanced existence. Celebrate the delight of nourishing yourself and your loved ones, knowing that each ingredient has been carefully selected to support not just the body but also the mind and spirit.

May this cookbook inspire you to explore, discover, and enjoy the joy of cooking as a kind of self-care and overall well-being. Use the culinary alchemy contained inside these pages to unleash the full taste of your wellness journey, and may each meal be a monument to the great potential that exists within each of us to flourish, one delicious mouthful at a time.

Bon appétit to a life well-nourished!